Somebody Hear Me Crying

Youth in Protective Services

A House Between Homes
Youth in the Foster Care System

A Different Way of Seeing
Youth with Visual Impairments and Blindness

The Ocean Inside
Youth Who Are Deaf and Hard of Hearing

My Name Is Not Slow
Youth with Mental Retardation

Chained
Youth with Chronic Illness

Runaway Train
Youth with Emotional Disturbance

Stuck on Fast Forward
Youth with Attention-Deficit/Hyperactivity Disorder

Why Can't I Learn Like Everyone Else?
Youth with Learning Disabilities

Finding My Voice
Youth with Speech Impairment

Somebody Hear Me Crying
Youth in Protective Services

Guaranteed Rights
The Legislation That Protects Youth with Special Needs

The Journey Toward Recovery
Youth with Brain Injury

Breaking Down Barriers
Youth with Physical Challenges

On the Edge of Disaster
Youth in the Juvenile Court System

The Hidden Child
Youth with Autism

Somebody Hear Me Crying

Me Crying

Youth in Protective Services

BY JOYCE LIBAL

MASON CREST PUBLISHERS

Mason Crest Publishers Inc.
370 Reed Road
Broomall, Pennsylvania 19008
(866) MCP-BOOK (toll free)

First printing
1 2 3 4 5 6 7 8 9 10
Library of Congress Cataloging-in-Publication Data on file at the Library of Congress.
ISBN 1-59084-739-3
1-59084-727-X (series)

Design by Harding House Publishing Service.
Composition by Bytheway Publishing Services, Inc., Binghamton, New York.
Cover art by Keith Rosko.
Cover design by Benjamin Stewart.
Produced by Harding House Publishing Service, Vestal, New York.
Printed and bound in the Hashemite Kingdom of Jordan.

Picture credits: Artville: pp. 20, 45; Corbis: p. 37; Photo Alto: pp. 24, 49, 59, 61, 62;
PhotoDisc: pp. 16, 17, 19, 21, 22, 38, 46, 47, 73, 76, 78, 86, 87, 92, 103, 105, 106,
107, 108, 117; PhotoSpin: pp. 33, 48, 71, 72, 74, 75, 89, 91, 101, 115, 118, 119, 120.
Individuals in Photo Alto and PhotoDisc images are models; all images are intended for
illustrative purposes only.

CONTENTS

Introduction   7

1. Ryan's World   11

2. Saturday Diversion   27

3. A Job and a "Friend"   41

4. Noticing Ryan   53

5. What's Next?   65

6. Coming Together   81

7. Helping Hands   97

8. A New Beginning   111

Further Reading   122
For More Information   123
Glossary   124
Index   126

A child with special needs is not defined by his disability.
It is just one part of who he is.

INTRODUCTION

Each child is unique and wonderful. And some children have differences we call special needs. Special needs can mean many things. Sometimes children will learn differently, or hear with an aid, or read with Braille. A young person may have a hard time communicating or paying attention. A child can be born with a special need, or acquire it by an accident or through a health condition. Sometimes a child will be developing in a typical manner and then become delayed in that development. But whatever problems a child may have with her learning, emotions, behavior, or physical body, she is always a person first. She is not defined by her disability; instead, the disability is just one part of who she is.

Inclusion means that young people with and without special needs are together in the same settings. They learn together in school; they play together in their communities; they all have the same opportunities to belong. Children learn so much from each other. A child with a hearing impairment, for example, can teach another child a new way to communicate using sign language. Someone else who has a physical disability affecting his legs can show his friends how to play wheelchair basketball. Children with and without special needs can teach each other how to appreciate and celebrate their differences. They can also help each other discover how people are more alike than they are different. Understanding and appreciating how we all have similar needs helps us learn empathy and sensitivity.

In this series, you will read about young people with special needs from the unique perspectives of children and adolescents who are experiencing the disability firsthand. Of course, not all children with a particular disability are the same as the characters in the stories. But the stories demonstrate at an emotional level how a special need impacts a child, his family, and his friends. The factual material in each chapter will expand your horizons by adding to your knowledge about a particular disability. The series as a whole will help you understand differences better and appreciate how they make us all stronger and better.

—*Cindy Croft*
Educational Consultant

YOUTH WITH SPECIAL NEEDS provides a unique forum for demystifying a wide variety of childhood medical and developmental disabilities. Written to captivate an adolescent audience, the books bring to life the challenges and triumphs experienced by children with common chronic conditions such as hearing loss, mental retardation, physical differences, and speech difficulties. The topics are addressed frankly through a blend of fiction and fact. Students and teachers alike can move beyond the information provided by accessing the resources offered at the end of each text.

   This series is particularly important today as the number of children with special needs is on the rise. Over the last two decades, advances in pediatric medical techniques have allowed children who have chronic illnesses and disabilities to live longer, more functional lives. As a result, these children represent an increasingly visible part of North American population in all aspects of daily life. Students are exposed to peers with special needs in their classrooms, through extracurricular activities, and in the community. Often, young people have misperceptions and unanswered questions about a child's disabilities—and more important, his or her *abilities*. Many times, there is no vehicle for talking about these complex issues in a comfortable manner.

This series provides basic information that will leave readers with a deeper understanding of each condition, along with an awareness of some of the associated emotional impacts on affected children, their families, and their peers. It will also encourage further conversation about these issues. Most important, the series promotes a greater comfort for its readers as they live, play, and work side by side with these individuals who have medical and developmental differences—youth with special needs.

—Dr. Lisa Albers, Dr. Carolyn Bridgemohan, Dr. Laurie Glader
Medical Consultants

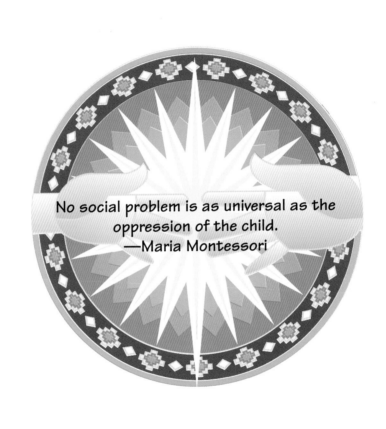

No social problem is as universal as the
oppression of the child.
—Maria Montessori

1

RYAN'S WORLD

Ryan lay motionless on his back with his arms stretched straight at his sides. He was intent on his personal ***ritual***.

Ryan was awake, yet he kept his eyes closed while listening to the sound of the gentle spring rain pelting the roof above his bedroom. Taking several deep breaths, he began first to erase all thoughts from his mind and then to slowly and selectively place images on the empty space. Chocolate chip cookies came first.

Ryan imagined the tantalizing aroma of warm chocolate chip cookies. He could see his mother bending over the shiny new stove, lifting the cookie sheet from the oven. . . .

She turned and smiled toward Ryan as she set the tray of steaming cookies on the island in the center of the spotless kitchen. Ryan poured two tall glasses of cold milk and carried them to the lace-covered table. He and his mother laughed and joked as they enjoyed this after-school snack while gazing through large French doors into the flower-filled yard. Mom rose as the back door opened and Ryan's father stepped into the sun-filled room.

"How was the office today, Honey?" she asked as her lips touched Tom Delaney's stubbly cheek.

"Fine, the Smith case has been a challenge, but I think I have every-

thing under control now," he replied. "I see you've been busy." Tom chuckled while glancing at the counter filled with cookies before turning toward his son. "How was school today, Ryan? I know you were worried about that science test."

"I think I aced it," Ryan said. "Thanks for going over the pretest with me last night. It really helped."

Tom Delaney set his briefcase beside a chair as he joined Ryan at the kitchen table. "Congratulations! I'm always here for you, son. Don't ever be afraid to ask for my help when you need it."

Debra Delaney returned with another glass and filled it with milk for her husband.

"Thanks, Dad. You're the best," Ryan responded. "I've been meaning to tell you that I'm thinking of going out for wrestling. The coach visited our gym class last week and told us a lot about the program. He said that two of last year's seniors even got college scholarships. I'm strong, and I think I could be pretty good at it. What do you think?"

Tom smiled and patted his son on the back. "Don't worry about college; we have money set aside for that. But I think wrestling sounds fantastic. I'm really proud of you, Ryan."

"I know you'll be good at anything you put your mind to, Ryan," his mother added. "And your father and I will have a great time cheering you on at the matches."

A loud clap of thunder brought Ryan back to reality. The gentle rain became a raging thunderstorm as he struggled to release his fantasy, open his eyes, and get out of bed. He sat up just in time to notice a mouse scurry under the chest of drawers.

I hate mice, was the first real thought of Ryan's new day, and he felt it was appropriate to his situation in life. Ryan didn't own a large wardrobe, and the clothes he did have lay dirty and scattered across the stained carpet. Selecting the least offensive of the lot, he dressed without bothering to take a shower.

The smell of cat urine grew more noticeable as Ryan opened the bedroom door and called Butch. "Do your duty," he ordered as he picked up the large gray cat and placed him inside the bedroom; then Ryan closed his bedroom door and stepped into the small hall. Ryan didn't bother to walk quietly down the hallway because he knew his father had been called in to work, and no amount of noise was ever great enough to wake his mom.

Sitting on the ripped upholstery-covered seat of a kitchen chair, he contemplated the room and felt defeat sink through his body. Dirty dishes were piled high in the sink and across the counter. Food-encrusted pots and pans were tumbled on each other on the old stove, and an open garbage bag had belched much of its contents across the soiled linoleum floor.

Ryan took a deep breath, gathered his courage, and rose to begin washing dishes. His growling stomach reminded him how hungry he was, but he had already eaten enough meals in the middle of this mess during the preceding week; he didn't want to eat again while staring at the mess.

When Debra Delaney entered the kitchen in the early afternoon, the dishes were done, the garbage was back in the bag, and Ryan had made a pot of coffee. The thirteen-year-old had not acquired a taste for the beverage, but he knew how much his mother liked it . . . and he hoped it would keep her from looking for something else to drink.

"Morning, Mom. I made scrambled eggs for you. Would you like toast to go with them?"

"Aren't you a sweet boy," his mother exclaimed. "I'll skip the toast, though. Just the eggs and some coffee will be fine." Ryan saw the worried look that skipped briefly across his mother's face as she brushed aside the unpaid bills that lay scattered across the tabletop. As he set the plate and cup before her, Debra's arm was stretched beyond the sleeve of her robe, and Ryan couldn't help but notice a new set of bruises. "That smells wonderful, Ryan." She took a bite. "And it tastes even better than it smells. I'm lucky to have you. In fact, what would I do without you?" She stared blankly at the peeling wallpaper beyond the table's edge, as though contemplating an empty life without Ryan.

"I'm not going anywhere," Ryan reminded her. "So you can stop worrying about that."

"Where's your father?" Debra looked anxiously around the room, as though she had just remembered her husband.

"He was called in to work by that temporary employment agency. Don't you remember? They phoned a couple of days ago."

"Yes, of course, I remember now." Ryan knew she was lying. She had so much trouble remembering things lately.

A noise from Ryan's room caught her attention. "What in the world is that?"

"Oh, that's Butch. I think he's catching a mouse."

"A mouse. Do we have mice?" Debra sounded surprised.

A crazy thought flashed across Debra's mind as she pictured the cat pouncing on the mouse and then flipping the stunned and helpless creature through the air. For a second the mouse seemed to have her face—while the cat looked an awful lot like her husband Tom.

Shaking the foolish image from her head, she said, "I'm sorry, Ryan, but will you go in there and see if the mouse is still alive? If it is, please take it away from Butch and set it free in the alley."

"Okay, if you say so." Her son looked surprised and puzzled, but he disappeared into his room, then returned a second later. "It's too late."

But Debra had already forgotten the mouse. "It sounds like the rain is letting up," she said to herself. "And look." She gazed out the grimy kitchen window. "The sun is trying to break free of the clouds. I think it's getting nicer. You should go outside and get some fresh air, Ryan."

"What about you? What are you going to do? Are you sure you'll be okay here alone?" She heard the concern in Ryan's voice.

"I'll be fine. I'm going to see what's on television. You just go on now."

Ryan went out the door, and she listened as his footsteps became quieter with each step down the stairs. She rose from her chair and watched from the window as Ryan crossed the alley. When he disappeared from sight, she walked to her bedroom and reached under the bed for the bottle of brandy that was hidden there. Returning to the kitchen, she poured some of the brandy into a glass and then carried both the glass and the bottle to the small living room. She stumbled over a pair of shoes but regained her balance without spilling a drop. Smiling at her cleverness, she snapped on the television and pulled a pile of laundry off the chair. The cushion was tipped on an angle, and Debra could see springs popping through the ripped seat lining. *This old thing has certainly seen better days*, she thought while placing the cushion at its proper angle. With a sigh, she plopped down and took a long swallow from the glass in her hand.

"This is Tuscany at its best," the television host pronounced.

Is that part of the real world? Do those people really exist? Are they actually eating fabulous food in that beautiful restaurant? Debra wondered as the alcohol slid down her throat. *What kind of lives do they live when the television camera is turned off and they go home? Are their houses beautiful? Do all the husbands love their wives? Do they have the money to buy anything they want and travel anywhere they'd like to go?*

As the afternoon wore on, Debra sank deeper into depression as the level of brandy in the bottle grew lower. As she fell into a drunken sleep, she had one last conscious thought. *I wonder where Ryan is. . . .*

SOME FACTS ABOUT CHILD ABUSE AND NEGLECT

- Each year, child welfare offices in the United States receive between two and three million reports of child abuse and neglect.
- Every day, at least three children are killed through abuse or neglect that is caused by their parent(s) or a person who is caring for them.
- At least 75 percent of the children who die because of abuse or neglect are less than five years old.
- Children are abused in between 30 and 60 percent of homes where domestic violence occurs.
- Every year approximately 18,000 children become disabled as a result of abuse or neglect.
- Substance abuse is involved in between one-third and two-thirds of the incidents of child abuse and child neglect.
- As many as 80 percent of parents who abuse their children were once the victims of child abuse.
- Some studies have found that the majority of individuals in prisons were abused as children.

ALL CHILDREN HAVE A RIGHT TO BE SAFE

Both federal and state laws define child abuse and neglect. Laws concerning child abuse and neglect refer to children who are under the age of eighteen. Federal legislation, specifically the Child Abuse Prevention and Treatment Act, defines the minimum guidelines that must be used by states in forming their own definitions of child abuse and neglect. A state's definition of child abuse and neglect determines when it is legal for the state to intervene in a family in order to provide protection for a child. The exact wording in the definition of child abuse and neglect varies from one state to another. For example, some states use the words "harm or threatened harm" in their definitions, while other states add the word "serious" as a prefix to that phrase. Seemingly small differences—like just one word—can have a large impact when determining whether or not a behavior is within the law.

WHAT IS CHILD ABUSE?

When a parent or other person who is caring for a child causes nonaccidental physical or emotional injury to the child, it is called child abuse.

Physical Abuse

This can take many forms, including but not limited to:

- kicking
- punching
- hitting
- burning
- cutting
- sexual abuse

Emotional Abuse

This too can take many forms, including but not limited to:

- humiliation
- degradation
- unduly severe criticism
- excessive isolation
- causing extreme guilt
- causing fear or terror
- sexual abuse

WHAT IS NEGLECT?

According to current laws in North America, parents must provide their children with certain necessities, including food, clothing, shelter, and medical treatment. Parents who do not provide these things are guilty of physical neglect.

A child may also suffer emotional neglect and educational neglect.

Physical Neglect

This includes but is not limited to:

- abandonment
- lack of proper nourishment
- lack of parental supervision
- lack of medical care
- lack of proper hygiene
- failure to provide adequate clothing and shelter

People who have been the victims of abuse or neglect may keep the secrets of their childhood into adulthood. They feel a tremendous pressure "not to tell."

Emotional neglect can be as serious as physical neglect.

Emotional Neglect

This includes but is not limited to:

- rejection
- failure to nurture
- lack of affection
- failure to comfort in times of stress

Educational Neglect

This includes:

- failure to provide an opportunity to receive adequate schooling
- allowing truancy

When an investigation proves that child abuse or neglect is occurring in a home, states are required to make *reasonable efforts* to allow the child to remain with his family or to

return the child to the home after foster care. The Adoption and Safe Families Act makes clear, however, that the **paramount** concern when making these decisions is the *health and safety of the child*. Rather than remove a child from the home, sometimes the court might issue an order of protection requiring that the person who has caused harm be removed from the home, thus allowing the child to remain there.

POSSIBLE SIGNS OF CHILD ABUSE OR NEGLECT

Sometimes abused or neglected children do not exhibit any outward signs of this treatment. Other times, signs are present. While the following conditions do not necessarily indicate child abuse or neglect, the presence of one or more of

them, especially when observed on more than one occa-
sion, might be an indicator that the child and family could
benefit from intervention by social services:

- burns
- cuts
- bruises
- swelling
- bite marks
- bald spots
- untreated medical problems
- fear that appears excessive for a given situation
  (especially fear of a parent's reaction)
- difficulty walking or sitting
- low self-esteem
- chronic fatigue
- inappropriate dress for the weather (for example: not
  being dressed warmly enough in winter or wearing
  long sleeves in warm weather to cover abuse marks
  on arms)
- unkempt appearance
- an obvious need for dental work
- some speech disorders
- malnourished appearance
- unsupervised young child
- infantile behavior in an older child
- truancy
- exaggerating minor pain
- denying major pain
- aggressive and destructive behavior
- extreme shyness or passive behavior
- substance abuse
- running away from home
- sexual behavior that is exhibited by a young
  child

Teachers may observe signs of abuse or neglect in their students.

ADULT BEHAVIORS THAT MAY INDICATE A PARENT OR CARETAKER ABUSES OR NEGLECTS THE CHILD IN HIS OR HER CARE

- substance abuse (or providing a child with illegal substances)
- humiliating a child in front of others
- failure to provide medical treatment for a child who is in need of these services
- ignoring a child who is asking for emotional support or affection
- punishing a child in a way that seems excessive (for example, isolating a child for prolonged periods of time)
- unduly severe criticism of a child
- threatening a child
- failure to supervise children
- missed appointments with teachers or doctors

It is not attention the child is seeking but love.
—Sigmund Freud

2

SATURDAY DIVERSION

Ryan wiped the image of his mother further from his mind with each step as he descended the stairs and stepped into the alley. A dog barked, and Ryan glanced up at the balcony that held the chained animal. *You can't get me, you poor old thing,* he thought while noticing the assortment of plastic and metal lawn chairs, garbage bags, and laundry sprinkled across other balconies that faced the alley.

As he stepped around the corner and onto the street, he wondered about all the people who lived behind the balconies. *It's funny how downtown buildings have sides that look so different from each other,* he thought. The front of his building was composed of sand-colored bricks with pretty blue and white striped awnings above the windows. The downstairs housed an old-fashioned barbershop with one of those striped barber poles in front of it. All the buildings on Ryan's street had fancy fronts; but the alley was something else, and Ryan was curious about the things that were taking place behind the facades.

From his own balcony, he sometimes watched people going in and out of their apartments, and he believed these observations had made him a good judge of character. He didn't like the man with the dog because he was loud, and Ryan had witnessed his cruelty. Dog-man would yell obscenities at his pet and often kicked it, turning the dog into a mean and sullen beast. Another apartment held a sweet old grandmother. Ryan knew because he had seen her kissing two little girls good-bye one Sunday. "Bye, Grandma," they called from the car window just before their parents drove them out of the alley. Ryan imagined that Grandma kept her apartment as neat as a pin and that she baked goodies for those two little girls. "Lovers" was what Ryan secretly called the young couple who lived in the apartment across the alley from his own. Lover-man and lover-woman always walked down the stairs together and kissed good-bye before getting into separate cars and driving off to work. Ryan was positive that lover-woman and lover-man ate nice meals together and sat close to each other while holding hands when they watched television. Ryan suspected that another apartment housed a drug dealer because all manner of people went in and out of it day and night, and no one ever stayed there very long.

Pushing his neighbors out of his mind, Ryan bent his head and got down to business. He didn't get an allowance, so every Saturday he prowled a regular route in search of change that had spilled out of pockets and purses during the week. He had discovered that many people either didn't notice or didn't bother to bend down to pick up the nickels and dimes they dropped while trying to insert them into parking meters, especially if the change rolled under a car. That was good news for Ryan because most Saturdays he could gather enough money to meet his friends at Bob's Pizzeria. They'd play a couple video games, or shoot a game of pool, and often have a slice or two of pizza before returning home.

Most Saturdays, Ryan would eat a quick bowl of cereal and be out the door and on change patrol early in the morning. Today, however, he'd gotten a late start because of doing the dishes and cooking eggs. He'd never be able to gather enough money for a slice of pizza. *Oh well, I have enough for one video game*, he decided. *I'll just say I'm not hungry.*

"Where were you?" Will asked when Ryan arrived at Bob's.

"Yeah, what took you so long?" Jimmy chimed in.

"Sorry," Ryan responded. "I got up late."

"Well, I've already spent most of my allowance while we were waiting for you," Jimmy complained. "I only have enough left for one slice of pizza."

"Actually, I don't think I'm hungry enough for pizza today. I'll just sit with you guys while you eat," Ryan responded.

"Oh come on," Will said. "My dad gave me extra money this week. Let me treat both of you to pizza. I even have enough to buy soda."

"Okay, I guess I could eat a little," Ryan agreed.

Will ate his slice of pizza slowly while watching Ryan wolf down his serving. A satisfied smile curled the corners of Ryan's lips as he washed down the last of the pizza. "So that's what you eat like when you're *not* hungry," Jimmy observed, and the three boys laughed.

"I guess maybe I was hungrier than I thought," admitted Ryan as he noticed the intent look on Will's face. "What's the matter with you?"

"Oh, nothing, sorry."

Will was trying to hide his growing curiosity about Ryan, but he was beginning to discover Ryan's secrets. Three weeks ago, Will had been in the car with his mother when they passed Ryan. Will was about to call out to his friend, but something stopped him—maybe it was Ryan's posture, because his head was bent forward and he was searching the ground intently. When Will saw Ryan stoop to pick up a coin and place it in his pocket, a lightbulb went off in Will's mind. *So this is how Ryan gets his money for Saturday afternoons at Bob's,* he thought. The pieces were starting to fall together.

Ryan had started attending Franklin Middle School about a year ago. He, Will, and Jimmy had become friends almost immediately, but neither Will nor Jimmy knew much about Ryan's life other than the fact that he was an only child. Both Will and Jimmy lived on the residential side streets that skirted the main streets in this section of town. It was about a seven-block walk for Will to get to Bob's Pizzeria; it was a little farther for Jimmy, so he usually rode his bike. Ryan had visited both Will and Jimmy at their houses, but he never invited them to his own home. Ryan said that his mom was sick and that it wouldn't be any fun going there. But Will was starting to suspect that Ryan was ashamed of wherever he lived.

Will wasn't really sure what had made him suspicious of Ryan's stories, but one day a couple of months back, he decided to follow Ryan home. Will's mom had taken him to the dentist late in the morning, and by the time his appointment was over, there were only a couple hours left in the school day. Will convinced his mother to let him skip the rest of school, and when Ryan got off the school bus that afternoon, Will was hiding in the bushes at the edge of the apartment complex. He watched intently as Ryan walked down the sidewalk toward the back of the first apartment building and turned as if to enter the courtyard. But instead of doing that, Ryan sat on a bench just outside the courtyard and waited while the other kids who had gotten off the bus disappeared down their own streets or into the apartment buildings. When they were out of sight, he picked up his backpack and continued walking. Racing from one clump of bushes or trees to another, Will kept his distance so as not to be discovered as he followed his friend. Ryan finally turned into the alley behind the buildings on Main Street, and Will hid around the corner of the nearest building while he watched Ryan ascend the stairs to his hidden home.

Will didn't mention his new knowledge to anyone, but he thought about it a lot, and he had begun to piece the mystery of Ryan's life together. Ryan had obviously lied about being hungry. Will wondered why.

Anxiety overtook Ryan each time it was time to go home. He really liked Jimmy and Will, and he enjoyed being with them on Saturdays. Ryan was engaged in a never-ending struggle to ***suppress***

worry, and being with friends helped him accomplish that. But worry grew to be a constant and unwelcome companion whenever he returned home.

Today was no exception. It was starting to rain again as Ryan mounted the stairs that led to his apartment, and the dreary weather matched his mood. "Mom," he called as he opened the door.

No answer greeted him. Ryan didn't bother to close the door as his eyes went from the tipped liquor bottle on the living room floor to his mother, who lay slouched in the chair beside it. "Mom!" he called, rushing to grab his mother's limp hand.

He didn't hear the heavy footsteps coming up the stairs, and he almost screamed when someone grabbed him from behind and lifted his body from the floor.

WHY DO SOME PARENTS AND CAREGIVERS ABUSE OR NEGLECT CHILDREN?

Child abuse and neglect occur in every economic class, at every educational level, and among all ethnic groups. It is difficult to understand why some parents and caregivers engage in this behavior, and there are no circumstances under which it is okay for them to do so. There are certain conditions, however, that sometimes (but not always) foster child abuse and neglect. They include:

- extreme frustration
- uncontrolled stress
- lack of education
- unemployment
- poverty
- alcoholism
- drug abuse
- growing up without a good parental model
- being abused or neglected as a child
- isolation caused by lack of friendships
- lack of good extended-family relationships
- mental health problems
- some cultural backgrounds

EXEMPTIONS WRITTEN INTO THE LAWS REGARDING CHILD ABUSE AND NEGLECT

Certain exemptions are specified in some state laws regarding what constitutes child abuse. For example, a common exemption exists for members of certain religious groups who do not believe in medical care. In some cases, cultural practices are also exempt from the law. Even poverty and corporal punishment receive an exemption in some areas.

Some laws make an effort to define what is not allow-

Federal laws protect children from abuse, but the states are allowed to define what specific behaviors constitute abuse.

able corporal punishment, however. For example, a law might state that only spanking performed in a "reasonable manner" will not be considered child abuse. Other laws stipulate that any bruises or other injuries that are caused to a child by corporal punishment are considered child abuse.

THE HISTORY OF CHILD ABUSE AND EFFORTS TO PROTECT CHILDREN

- In ancient times children were sometimes killed as a ceremonial sacrifice to gods.
- Not so long ago, even in North America, children were considered to be the property of their fathers. Some parents who had many children might kill or abandon a newborn because they knew they would not be able to obtain enough food for another child.

Even a hundred years ago, children did not have the legal protection they do today. Many children were homeless or suffered from serious neglect due to their family's poverty.

Until recently, hitting a child with a stick, a hairbrush, or a belt was considered acceptable forms of punishment for misdemeanors.

- In 1646, Massachusetts passed the Stubborn Child Act, making it legal for parents to beat their children to death for being disobedient, lazy, or even rude.
- In the 1700s, the Virginia Colony enacted laws protecting **apprenticed children** from harsh treatment by the people employing them.
- In 1860, Dr. Ambroise Tardieu, a French physician, performed many autopsies on children whose deaths had been ruled accidental and determined that in many cases the real causes of death were burns or beatings.
- In 1863, Franklin B. Sanborn became the executive secretary of the Massachusetts State Board of Charities. Sanborn established a "visitors'" program that consisted of upper- and middle-class women visiting

the poor for the purpose of instructing them in budgeting and parenting skills and encouraging sobriety.

- In 1875, Eldridge T. Gerry, an attorney, established the New York Society for the Prevention of Cruelty to Children.
- In 1899, Illinois created the first true juvenile court, which was presided over by Judge Merritt Pinckney.
- In 1935, Congress passed the Social Security Act, which called for the protection of homeless, dependent, and neglected children.
- In 1938, Congress passed the Fair Labor Standards Act, making it illegal for children under the age of sixteen to work all day in factories and mines.
- In 1946, Dr. John Caffey began using X-ray machines as a tool to detect bones that had not healed properly in children. When broken bones are not reported to medical practitioners, they remain untreated and may not heal correctly. This is a sign of *probable* child abuse.
- In the 1960s, the *Journal of the American Medical Association* published a paper by Dr. C. Henry Kempe that described the **medical indicators** for child abuse. State legislatures in all fifty states passed laws making it illegal for parents to abuse their children. Congress demanded that all states provide welfare services to needy children.
- In 1974, Congress passed the Child Abuse Prevention and Treatment Act, which established the National Center on Child Abuse and Neglect under the Department of Health, Education, and Welfare and funded more than sixty programs and research studies.

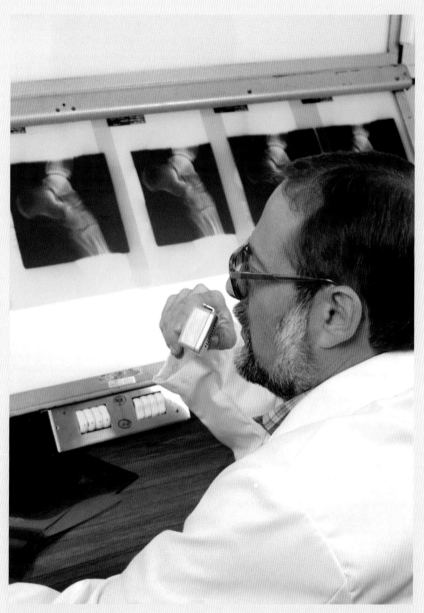

*X rays and other imaging technology help doctors to detect
signs of probable child abuse.*

- In 1980, Congress passed the Adoption Assistance and Child Welfare Act, which increased services offered to families in an effort to prevent the necessity of removing children from their homes.
- In 1993, Congress passed the Family Preservation and Family Support Act, encouraging agencies to form partnerships as an aid to identifying community needs regarding family support and preservation services.
- In 1997, Congress passed the Adoption and Safe Families Act, which required states to provide services to the families of at-risk children in order to make it possible for more children to remain with their families or to be reunited with them after foster care.

The American Congress has passed laws that protect children's safety.

- Even today, extreme poverty can cause parents to commit desperate acts. In some countries, children are still sold into slavery. There have been reported cases of parents purposely crippling or blinding their children in an effort to make them look more pitiful, so they can earn more money as beggars.

Children are people.
—Joseph Joubert

3

A Job and a "Friend"

Ryan raised his heavy, aching head from the carpet. Something warm and wet met his fingertips as he touched the sore spot on his forehead. Pulling his hand away, he realized that blood now dotted the tips of three fingers. His father's booming voice brought Ryan's attention back to the scene before him.

"What's the matter with you, Debra?" his father yelled. "I work all day, and you drink all day? You should have cleaned this pigsty! I'm tired and hungry!" It seemed to Ryan like his father's arms moved in slow motion as his left hand grabbed Debra by the robe and lifted her from the chair, while his right hand met her cheek with a loud smack.

"Tom!" she shrieked as she woke up.

"Dad!" Ryan grabbed his father's arm. Tears clogged the words in his throat. "Please don't hurt her. I asked Mom if I could make dinner for you tonight," he lied.

Tom Delaney's attention was riveted on his wife, and he gave no indication that he even heard his son until Ryan continued, "Dad, the barbershop is still open; someone's going to hear you."

Debra's limp body fell back into the chair as Tom released her and turned to face his son. "Make dinner then," he snarled and stomped off to the bathroom.

Ryan and Debra sat in silence for a moment. The sound of the shower made them realize they had a few minutes to compose themselves.

"Mom, hurry and get dressed so you'll look better when he gets out," Ryan pleaded.

"Look at you. You're bleeding," she mumbled.

Ryan pulled her from the chair and nudged her toward the bedroom. While Debra dressed, he grabbed hot dogs and French fries from the freezer. By the time his father came out of the bathroom, Ryan had supper on the table.

The family ate their meal in silence, and no one spoke again that evening.

Before he fell asleep that night, Ryan imagined that he and his loving parents had shared great conversation while eating a delicious pot roast for dinner. . . .

Ryan got home from Bob's Pizzeria just as his dad was returning from a day at the office. They met outside in the alley, and they could smell the pot roast as they walked up the stairs together. Tom opened the apartment door quietly, snuck up behind his wife, and kissed the side of her neck. Debra turned with a start, then laughed and hit her husband playfully with the dishtowel she held in her hands. His parents hugged, then pulled Ryan into their shared embrace. . . .

"What happened to you?" Will asked Ryan on Monday morning. He pointed to the cut and bruise on Ryan's forehead.

"Oh, it's nothing. I tripped and fell." Ryan thought Will's gaze was suspicious, but Ryan turned away before Will could say anything more.

Ryan's father was scheduled to work at the lumberyard all week, which was a relief to Ryan; he didn't have to worry about whether or not his mother was being hurt during the day. Debra had sent Ryan to the store after school on Monday, and he'd bought several foods that would be quick to cook, so he could have dinner waiting when his dad got home.

He was glad when Saturday rolled around, and he rose early to go on change patrol.

Mr. Walsh, who ran the barbershop, had been watching Ryan's Saturday activity for some time. Mr. Walsh had never met Ryan, but his interest in him had begun to grow in the past few weeks. One of the reasons why Ryan's Saturdays were so profitable was that Mr. Walsh had been purposely dropping coins on the block so Ryan could find them. This Saturday he planned to introduce himself to Ryan and make the boy an offer he couldn't refuse.

When Ryan stooped to pick up the dollar bill that was held down with a stone in front of the barbershop, Mr. Walsh stepped outside and asked, "How would you like to make one of those every day?"

"What do you mean?"

"I could use a little help in the shop. If you'd like to sweep up and clean the sinks each weekday and Saturday at about six o'clock, I'll pay you a dollar a day. It won't take up much of your time."

"Wow." For a moment Ryan seemed unable to say anything further. "That would be great," he said at last. "When do you want me to start? Hey, do you know that I live above your shop? My name is Ryan Delaney. Do you own this building?"

"No, I didn't know you lived here. I don't own the building, but I've rented this space for years. It's nice to meet you. My name is Peter Walsh, and you can start this afternoon."

"Great." Ryan's grin lit his face. "I'll see you at six."

Ryan couldn't wait to get to Bob's Pizzeria so he could share the news with Will and Jimmy. And over the next few weeks, his affection for Mr. Walsh grew. The barber did other cleaning while Ryan swept the floor and scoured the sinks. As they worked, Mr. Walsh always asked Ryan how school had gone, and Ryan told him about the events of the day.

It was really nice to have someone to talk to. Ryan even began sharing a little about his home life. He didn't tell Mr. Walsh that his mother drank most days and wasn't in any condition to hear about school when he got home. Instead, he said that his mother was sick and often wasn't feeling well enough to talk to him. He also didn't tell Mr. Walsh that his father didn't have a steady job or that he sometimes hit his wife and, on rare occasions, his son. Instead, Ryan just said that sometimes his father had a bad temper. Mr. Walsh was always sympathetic. He'd often place his arm around Ryan and say things like, "It's always darkest before the dawn," and "This too shall pass." That made Ryan feel better.

He was really happy to have Mr. Walsh for a friend—until the day that everything changed.

Mr. Walsh had been even nicer than normal that week—twice he gave Ryan an extra dollar, and every day they shared a candy bar after finishing work. "Say, Ryan," Mr. Walsh began that Friday as he broke the candy bar in half. "I've been meaning to show you something." He handed a magazine to Ryan.

Ryan's eyes grew wide with shock and his mouth dropped open. The boys in the magazine photos were naked.

WHAT IS SEXUAL ABUSE?

Children who are abused sexually each year may number in the hundreds of thousands. According to some **statistics**, the average age of a sexually abused child is eleven years old. While the majority of children suffering sexual abuse are girls, boys are also victimized in this manner.

Sometimes, sexual abuse is committed by strangers. According to statistics, these individuals often abuse more than sixty children before they are finally arrested. However, most sexual abuse is *not* committed by strangers. Sadly, parents and other caretakers are sometimes the perpetrators of sexual abuse.

When sexual abuse is present, family members may refuse to see, hear, or speak of this destructive secret.

Depending on the age of the child and circumstances under which the following take place, any of these activities may constitute sexual abuse:

- not allowing a child to have privacy while dressing (for example, requiring that a child keep the bedroom or bathroom door open when bathing or changing clothes).
- exposing a child to the nakedness or sexual acts of others (for example, forcing a child to shower with an adult or showing a child sexually explicit photos).
- asking a child to remove his clothing or to perform sexual acts.
- taking photographs of naked children.
- forcing a child to participate in any unwanted touching or kissing, or tricking a child into participating in inappropriate touching or kissing.

A child's innocence should be valued and protected.

A child who has been sexually abused may feel guilty, but when sexual abuse is taking place, the older person is always the guilty party.

Sexual abuse can take other forms that are not listed here. Some people who abuse children sexually begin by initiating seemingly innocent activity but then gradually **escalate** their advances.

Older teenagers, as well as adults, can be guilty of sexual abuse. While most of the individuals who commit this crime are men, women may sometimes abuse children in this way.

Whenever an older person abuses a child, the adult is always the guilty person, and the child is always the innocent victim.

DANGER SIGNALS

Remain alert around anyone who engages in the following activities. Any of these things can be signals of sexual abuse:

- If someone asks you to do something that makes you feel uncomfortable.
- If someone threatens you when you resist an action.
- If someone tricks you into doing something that doesn't feel right to you.
- If someone bribes you into doing something that doesn't feel right to you.
- If someone tells you to keep an action or their conversation with you a secret.
- If someone makes you feel trapped.

Sexual abuse may lead to feelings of shame and depression.

Counselors sometimes use dolls to help young children communicate their history of abuse.

Appropriate kinds of kissing and hugging can be a strong and wonderful sign of love and affection in families. However, everyone, including you, has the right to *not* kiss or hug people if kissing and hugging doesn't feel comfortable. This includes not kissing or hugging relatives.

If you feel uncomfortable engaging in any activity, you have the *right* to say so. It can be difficult, but go ahead and tell the person (or a parent or someone else you trust) that you feel uncomfortable and that you don't want to engage in that activity any more.

Family hugs are wonderful ways to communicate love—but anytime you feel uncomfortable, for whatever reason, you have the right to say so.

WHAT SHOULD YOU DO IF YOU HAVE BEEN A VICTIM OF *SEXUAL ABUSE?*

- Don't be embarrassed.
- Realize that you *did not* make a mistake or do anything wrong.
- Seek help from a parent, teacher, neighbor, the police, or someone else that you trust.

Every child has the right to be safe, to be loved, to know
that his life is worth more than any monetary amount.
—Joanna Haley

4

NOTICING RYAN

Ryan lifted his eyes to the smile on Mr. Walsh's face. Then he threw the magazine to the floor. He heard the word "No!" come out of his mouth, but it didn't sound like his own voice—it sounded deep, and slow, and very far away. Mr. Walsh placed his hand on Ryan's arm. Ryan recoiled, jumped up, and raced for the door.

Mr. Walsh's laughter was still echoing through Ryan's head as he sat sobbing, hidden between two buildings down the street. There was no danger now, since Mr. Walsh had not followed him out of the building, yet Ryan was reluctant to leave this spot. He didn't want anyone to see his tears, and he wasn't ready to face all the problems in his life.

The late afternoon sunshine faded as thoughts crowded each other in Ryan's mind: *What's wrong with me? Why can't life be the same for me as it is for other kids? Why do I live in the alley instead of a house? Why does Mom drink? Why does Dad hurt us? Why is Mr. Walsh a pervert, and why did he pick me? Why can't I just be normal?*

When the tears finally stopped, Ryan dragged himself home. It was dark, and he was in trouble.

"Where were you?" Tom shouted at his son as he entered the kitchen.

"I'm sorry. I don't know it was so late. I was just thinking."

"You were *thinking*? You must have been doing more than just thinking!" His father glared at him. But Ryan didn't know how to respond. He didn't want to tell his dad about Mr. Walsh.

"I don't know. I really was just thinking," Ryan repeated.

"Well maybe you need to do some more thinking in your room." His father gave Ryan a shove.

Ryan lost his balance and stumbled against the kitchen counter. As his face hit the counter's edge, Ryan knew he'd end up with a bruise that he'd have to explain to Will and Jimmy tomorrow.

The next morning, Ryan's spirits lifted a little. He avoided the barbershop while on change patrol and he told Will and Jimmy all about Mr. Walsh that afternoon.

"Wow!" Jimmy exclaimed. "What a pervert!"

"What are you going to do? Did you tell your parents?" Will asked.

"No, I'm not going to tell anybody. I'm just going to stay away from him."

Will's face was screwed up in thought. "I don't know, it seems like you should tell somebody. Maybe you should call the police."

Ryan was surprised by Will's suggestion. "The police? I'm not calling the police! I just want to forget about it."

But Will couldn't forget about it any more than he could forget about the lump Ryan had on his forehead several weeks ago—or about the sore leg he had after that, or the black eye he had before it, or the bruised cheek he had today. Ryan always had an excuse for these injuries. He had fallen down the stairs, bumped into a door in the dark, slipped in the shower, tripped over the cat. . . . How could someone who never fell down or bumped into anything in Will's presence be so accident prone at home? Will was beginning to suspect there was another reason for all these injuries. He decided to talk to his parents about everything that evening.

"I'm glad you came to us with this, Will," his dad said. "Child **pornography** is a sad and serious thing. It is wrong of Mr. Walsh to own that kind of magazine, and it was certainly wrong for him to trick Ryan into looking at it. We are going to have to report this to the police. Will, I think you need to realize that we'll have to tell the police Ryan's name, and I'm sure the police will want to question him."

"Oh, no! He's going to know that I told and be mad at me."

"I'm afraid you may be right about that, son. But I'm sure Ryan won't be in any trouble, and I think he'll come to realize that you did the right thing," his father reassured him.

"What about the rest of it? What about his mom and dad?" Will asked.

"I don't know." His mother looked worried. "You didn't actually see either of them hurt Ryan, did you?"

"No, but I know they do it. How else does he end up hurt so often? And he never invites Jimmy or me to his house. I know it's because his parents are mean, and he doesn't want us to meet them."

"I just don't want to make any false accusations about anyone," his mother said. "There are good reasons to be suspicious, I agree, but I hate for us to get involved in something that we're not really sure about. It would be different if Ryan had actually told you that either his mother or his father had hurt him. Has he ever said that?"

"No, but I know they do it," insisted Will.

"Doesn't it seem strange that none of your teachers have noticed a problem?"

"When his forehead was hurt, he just let his hair hang down over it. When he's hurt, he hides it, or he gives some lame excuse for how it happened," Will explained.

"Let's sleep on it and discuss it again in the morning," his father suggested.

Will didn't go directly to bed, however. Instead, he walked over to the computer in his room and went on-line. He typed www.google.com into the bar at the top of the page and pressed GO. When the Google page came up on the screen, he typed "child abuse" and then pressed the words Google Search. That yielded more than two million listings, so he decided to narrow them down by adding the name of his state to child abuse and hitting search again. There were still hundreds of thousands of hits, but he began to scroll through the first ones and noticed the word "hotline" in some of them. Opening up one of those pages provided a toll-free telephone number that could be used to make **anonymous** reports of suspected child abuse or neglect. It also had surprising statistics regarding the number of abused and neglected children in his state and elsewhere in North America. Will printed that page and another that gave information on how to recognize some of the signs of child abuse. With this new information, he was confident he'd be able to convince his parents to make an anonymous telephone call to the hotline the next morning.

"Well." His father looked over the printed information. "I'm proud of you, Will. You really did your homework on this thing didn't you?"

"You see, it doesn't cost anything to make the call, and you don't even have to give your name," Will explained between bites of toast.

"I don't know. What do you think, Beth?" His father turned toward Will's mom.

She thought for a moment. "I guess we can just tell them about our suspicions. We'll simply say what Will has observed, and then it will be up to Child Protective Services to conduct an investigation and determine the facts. We don't have to actually accuse Ryan's parents of child abuse. Okay. Let's do it. I don't think it will hurt anything, and it might really help Ryan a lot."

Making the call turned out to be easy. The person at the hotline desk listened carefully and recorded all the information. When they hung up the phone, Will and his parents felt relieved and confident they had made the right decision.

Will and his family didn't know it, but someone else had also made a call to Child Protective Services regarding Ryan the previous evening.

WHAT IS CHILD PROTECTIVE SERVICES (CPS)?

According to federal and state law, children must be protected from abuse and neglect. The job of protecting children from these situations falls to the Departments of Child Protective Services, which are operated by the states. These offices are part of the Department of Social Services. Some states have a Department of Protective Services and a Department of Preventive Services. These offices are charged with making certain that children are safe and that their best interests and welfare are assured. While some individuals in the Child Protection Department have the authority to remove children from their home under certain circumstances, this is not done unless the safety and welfare of the child are in jeopardy. Through this branch of the welfare system, services can be provided not only to children who are abused and neglected but also to their families in order to assist them in correcting the situation.

WHEN AND HOW TO REPORT SUSPECTED CASES OF CHILD ABUSE OR NEGLECT

Most people do not like to get involved in unpleasant situations. Making the decision to phone in a report of suspected child abuse or neglect can be very agonizing. When we do not act to stop child abuse and neglect, however, we allow it to continue. Each of us must do everything possible to protect children. Remember that it is not your responsibility to prove that a child has been the victim of abuse or neglect when you make a report. You do not even have to be certain that abuse or neglect has taken place. It is only necessary that you suspect abuse or neglect in order to make the call. Not doing so may mean that a child will remain in danger and have new abuses committed against her. If you do

suspect that a child has been abused or neglected, you should definitely act to protect the child by making a simple telephone call.

You may call your local office of the Department of Social Services. There are also hotline telephone numbers that you may call. These lines are staffed twenty-four hours every day, so it is easy to make a call whenever it is convenient for you. Of course, if you suspect that a child is in danger, you should make the call immediately. You can also call the local police department twenty-four hours a day.

If you cannot locate the hotline number for your state, you can call the Childhelp USA® National Child Abuse Hotline toll-free at 1-800-4ACHILD (1-800-422-4453).

Can anyone report suspected child abuse or neglect, and what kinds of questions might be asked when doing so?

Yes, anyone, even children, can report suspected child abuse or neglect.

All situations are different, but the person answering the telephone call will want to obtain as much information as possible. While it is not necessary for you to give your name, you may decide to provide it. That way, people investigating the case will be able to contact you if they have more questions. Names of people reporting suspected child abuse or neglect are usually kept confidential and only released under a judge's orders. You can ask the person taking the call if your name will be kept **confidential**.

You will be asked information such as the child's name, age, sex, and address. You do not even have to have this much information in order to make the telephone call, however. For example, you may have witnessed harsh treatment of a child in a parking lot and only possess the license plate number of the car the child was in. Even with

A child who is being abused at home may be more apt to get in fights at school.

When a child is being abused, she may be unusually quiet or have difficulty concentrating at school.

this small bit of information, you can make a call that protects a child.

Of course, if you do have more information, such as the
name and address of the parents or caretakers of the child,
you will be asked to provide it. If the abuse was caused by
someone other than the parent or caretaker, and you know
the name of that person, you should give that information.

You will be asked to describe the abuse or neglect that
you have witnessed or the reasons why you suspect abuse
or neglect has taken place.

When we protect our children, we protect our future.
—Wilma Russell

5

WHAT'S NEXT?

Ryan returned home from Bob's Pizzeria to an all-too-familiar situation. Debra had spent the day drinking and Tom was furious. If Ryan had heard the glass break before entering the apartment, he might not have gone inside, but it was just as he opened the door that his father threw the liquor bottle across the room. Brandy flew in all directions.

Concern and fear gripped Ryan's heart when he didn't see his mother. Still poised on the threshold, he heard the words, "Where's Mom?" come out of his mouth, but they sounded strange, like the word "No!" did yesterday in the barbershop—deep, and slow, and far away.

Tom's voice was thick with disgust as he replied, "In the bedroom. She's drunk, and I'm not staying here while she sleeps it off." He shoved past his son.

Ryan closed the door behind his father and ran to find his mother. "Mom," he whispered. Now his voice sounded small and frail and filled with fear. Debra's chest rose ever so slightly and then subsided. Ryan took comfort from that small rhythmic movement.

He held her limp hand and said her name over and over. When there was no reaction, he lifted her head and peered more closely into her face. "Mom, Mom, please wake up," he pleaded. "Mom, please don't die. I'm scared. I don't know what to do."

A thought flashed across his mind—*911*. Springing from the bed, he dashed to the kitchen. His hand shook as he picked up the phone and pressed 911. "Hello, my name is Ryan Delaney and I need help." The words tumbled from his mouth. "I can't wake my mother. I think she's unconscious."

After obtaining Ryan's address and telephone number, the operator asked him a series of questions, and Ryan answered as best he could. "I'm thirteen." . . . "I think she's had a lot to drink." . . . "He's not home." . . . "I'm alone." The operator told Ryan to take the phone into his mother's bedroom. After Ryan assured her that Debra was still breathing, the operator instructed him to stay on the line until the ambulance arrived.

A few moments passed; then Ryan heard sirens in the distance. As the sound grew, he wondered briefly if he had done the right thing. That feeling was quickly taken over by relief, however, when the emergency medical technicians knocked on the door, entered the bedroom, and began to help his mother.

The response team took note of the condition of the apartment as they walked through it. The 911 operator had already informed them that the call came from a thirteen-year-old boy. After confirming that he had been left alone in the apartment with his unconscious mother, they strongly suspected that the family needed ***intervention*** from CPS.

"What's your name, son?" one of the technicians asked as he assessed Debra's condition. "Do you know how long your mom has been like this?"

"I'm Ryan. She was like this when I got home. That was about an hour ago, I guess. Is she going to be okay?"

"I think so. You did the right thing to call us, Ryan. We're going to take your mom to the hospital so the doctors can help her. I'd like you to ride along with us, okay?"

"Sure," Ryan agreed. "I want to stay with her."

Ryan was sitting in the waiting room and an emergency-room

doctor was examining Debra when the technicians reported the situation to the social service staff at the hospital. Ryan looked up at the **medical social worker** as she introduced herself and extended her hand. She immediately noticed his dark cheek. "That looks like a nasty bruise," she commented. "How did it happen?"

"I tripped and fell into the kitchen counter."

"I see." Ryan assured her that he didn't have any other injuries, but the EMTs had already told her several troubling things: the Delaney apartment reeked of cat urine, dirty dishes covered every counter, open garbage bags sat in the kitchen, floors were covered with filth, dirty laundry littered every room, and bottles of alcohol were easily accessible.

She wouldn't be able to speak to the boy's mother until morning, and it would probably be even later before the father was located and available. Ryan had immediate needs that neither his mother nor his father could satisfy. He was hungry, and he needed a safe place to spend the night.

Mr. Frie, the caseworker from CPS, arrived shortly after the social worker telephoned him. He interviewed Ryan, determined that no **extended family** was available to assist the child, and decided that since the mother was hospitalized and the father had not been located, CPS needed to take **temporary custody** of Ryan.

"Are you Ryan?" the doctor asked as she entered the waiting room. "Your mother is doing much better, but I want to keep her here overnight. She can't speak with you right now, but by tomorrow I expect she'll be anxious to talk to you."

"Thank you." The caseworker and Ryan responded at the same time. Mr. Frie then rose from his chair, introduced himself to the physician, explained that he was a caseworker from CPS, and continued. "I'm going to take Ryan for some food now, and I imagine he's getting pretty tired. I'll make sure that he's back here tomorrow afternoon so he can visit his mom."

Turning his attention back toward Ryan, Mr. Frie stooped down to Ryan's eye level and began to explain further: "It's the job of CPS to help kids. I can't take you back to your home tonight, but CPS operates a very nice ***receiving home*** where kids can spend a night or two or even more when it's necessary. Right now there are nine children staying there. I think this will be the best place for you to spend the night, Ryan, and I'll bring you back here tomorrow."

Ryan's head was filled with so many worries that he felt like it could explode:

Is Mom really okay? Why can't I see her tonight?

Why do I have to leave the hospital?

Where could Dad be? What's going to happen when he goes home and Mom and I aren't there? Will he be worried about us? He's going to be really mad at me for calling 911!

What if nobody brings me back here?

How long will Mom have to stay in the hospital?

When can I go home?

Ryan did not speak his worries aloud; he remained silent as Mr. Frie led him out of the hospital to his car. They stopped for a burger and fries before continuing on to the Jefferson County Receiving Home.

After Ryan had spent more time with Mr. Frie, however, he was able to speak some of his questions and concerns. Mr. Frie answered them and did his best to reassure Ryan that everything would be okay.

Ryan's stomach hurt, however, when they pulled up to the residential facility. It was dark, but what Ryan could see of the outside of the building looked nice. Ryan was used to pretty facades, however, so he was reserving judgment on the place until he saw the interior and met the people who lived and worked there.

Because of the late hour, the children in residence were in bed, and most of the staff had left for the day several hours ago. Only the night shift remained on duty. A motherly woman named Phyllis stepped out of the room immediately after meeting him and returned with pajamas, a toothbrush, shampoo, a towel—everything Ryan needed to prepare for the night. "After you're ready for bed, I'll take your clothes and wash them for you so they'll be nice and clean tomorrow morning," she said. "One other thing." She led him to a small closet and opened the door. "There's a group of ladies in town who make quilts for all the kids who stay here. We keep the quilts in this closet. You can pick out the one you like best, and it's yours to keep. Take it to your bed tonight, and take it with you when you go home."

Ryan thought this was kind of strange, but he selected a colorful quilt that was covered with stars. Later that night, he was happy to have his quilt. Even though he had just acquired it, it was comforting to have something that belonged to him in this strange place. He thought about the colors on the quilt as he tried to relax.

Then he imagined that his family had just purchased a brand new house and his bedroom was decorated in all the colors of his new quilt. That was why it felt strange to be here, he pretended: he was in his new bedroom, and it was still somewhat unfamiliar to him. Mom and Dad were sleeping in the next room, and Dad had promised to take him, Will, and Jimmy fishing in the morning. He'd better get some sleep now because tomorrow was going to be a big day. . . .

Mr. Frie was on a rotating schedule with other CPS caseworkers to respond to emergency calls during evening hours and on weekends. This Saturday night was his shift, which was why he was the first one to meet Ryan, who had now been added to his **caseload**.

Mr Frie was anxious to speak with both Mr. and Mrs. Delaney so that he could better assess the family's circumstances. Mr. Frie realized the first **hearing** concerning Ryan would take place in **juvenile court** within a couple of days, and he needed to be ready to make a recommendation to the judge.

The medical social worker was already meeting with Debra when Mr. Frie and Ryan arrived at the hospital on Sunday. After explaining to Ryan that he needed to speak with his mother and the social worker for a few minutes before Ryan could join them, Mr. Frie entered Debra's room.

Debra's first questions concerned her son: "Where is he? Has he been injured? Is he okay?" After being assured that Ryan was being cared for, she asked about her husband. She was glad to hear that Tom had been located, but she was worried about the possibility of seeing him.

"You don't have to see him now," the social worker explained. "There are services available to help you and your family, Mrs. Delaney." The social worker explained how the **battered women's shelter** operated.

But Debra blamed herself for her husband's rage. "I don't even remember when all of this started, but now it's all because of my drinking," she said tearfully. "I want to stop, but I just can't. I hate what I've become. I'm weak. I'm a terrible mother and an even worse wife."

"Does your husband ever hurt Ryan?" Mr. Frie asked.

"He doesn't mean to do it." Mrs. Delaney confirmed Mr. Frie's suspicion. "He just becomes so angry with me that he can't control himself."

"There are services available to help your husband, too, Mrs. Delaney," Mr. Frie responded. "I spoke with Mr. Delaney briefly by phone this morning, and I'm going to be meeting with him tomorrow. After that, I'll need to speak with you again."

"I want things to change. They have to." Debra was overcome with uncontrollable sobs as she continued, "There's something else. Neither Tom nor Ryan knows this, but I'm pregnant."

WHAT USUALLY HAPPENS WHEN A TELEPHONE CALL IS RECEIVED REGARDING SUSPECTED CHILD ABUSE OR NEGLECT

Reports are investigated by CPS. A caseworker will meet and interview the child. The individual who has been accused of abuse will not be present during this interview. The caseworker will also interview the parents or caregivers. Teachers and doctors might also be interviewed. If the investigation determines that abuse or neglect has occurred, CPS determines if allowing the child to remain in the home will put her in danger.

Children are not casually or routinely removed from their homes. This action is only taken when a child is at risk of

serious harm should she remain there. When it is necessary to remove a child from her home, efforts are made to solve problems so the family can be reunited.

If the person who made the initial report of suspected child abuse or neglect provided a name and address, he may receive a letter from CPS acknowledging the call, but he will not be given any information regarding the case or be informed of the outcome of any investigations, because such information is confidential.

By law, an investigation of the allegation must begin within a specified number of hours after a report has been made. The outcome of the investigation may not be required for some time, however—perhaps sixty days after the initial report was made.

If a child's home environment is not safe, that may constitute neglect.

A stuffed animal or a quilt is often provided to help a child feel more secure after she has been taken from her home.

A Typical Scenario

Within twenty-four hours, an investigation is under way by a trained caseworker from CPS. The caseworker speaks with the child in question and visits the home. In assessing the child's situation, the caseworker notes whether or not the home is safe and if food is available. The safety of other children who are found to be living in the home is also considered. The worker takes note of who else is living in the home and of the various types of activities that take place there. For example, the worker will be alert for drug and alcohol use.

If the worker finds that abuse or neglect has taken place, he makes a determination as to whether or not allowing the child to remain in the home constitutes a risk to the child. If it is determined that the child is in imminent danger should

he be allowed to remain in the home, the caseworker takes
the child into protective custody. (Often the caseworker will
consult with her supervisor before making this decision.) If
the child is removed from the home, the parents will usually
be told where the child is being taken. They will also be
informed of their right to attend court proceedings and to
request that the court return custody of the child to them.
Details of the investigation are entered into the state register.

The family situation is assessed and services to remedy
the causes of child abuse or neglect will be offered. The family is not legally bound to accept this advice from CPS, or to
participate in the suggested activities and services. The court
may decide to mandate participation by the family, however,
as a condition for the possible return of the child.

A teacher is required by law to report any suspicions she has that a child is being abused or neglected.

WHAT IS A *MANDATED* REPORTER?

A mandated reporter is a person who is obligated by law to report suspicion of child abuse or neglect. Mandated reporters are usually members of specific professions. If these individuals (through their professional roles) come to suspect that a child is a victim of abuse or neglect and fail to report it to the proper authorities, they can face prosecution for their omission. In many states, members of the following professions are among those designated as mandated reporters:

- doctors
- nurses
- emergency medical technicians
- psychologists
- teachers
- day-care workers
- dentists
- dental hygienists
- chiropractors
- *coroners*
- employees of social services
- law enforcement officers
- substance-abuse counselors

In some states *anyone* who knows that child abuse or neglect is occurring and does not report it is subject to a fine and possible imprisonment.

WHAT KINDS OF THINGS DOES THE OFFICE OF CHILD PROTECTIVE SERVICES DO?

- investigates *allegations* of abuse and neglect
- determines causes of abuse and neglect

- prevents further harm to children
- decides what is in the best interest of the children
- takes action to maximize the family's ability to keep the children safe in their own home
- removes children from abusive situations
- assumes custody of children when necessary
- provides a safe environment for children who are removed from home
- provides treatment for physical and mental harm that has taken place
- assists parents in correcting problems that have led to abuse and neglect of their children
- helps families learn how to care properly for their children
- offers referrals to other offices and organizations that can assist parents in correcting problems that have led to abuse

The Office of Child Protective Services may refer a child for other services as well, such as tutoring.

When it is necessary to remove a child from her home, it is usually the goal of CPS to assist in correcting the situation that necessitated removal of the child so that the child can be returned home as soon as possible.

While the child is out of the parents' home, CPS assures that the child is safe and properly cared for either in a foster home or in other residential care.

When it is not possible to return a child to the care of the biological parents, CPS works to have parental rights terminated and to find permanent placement (such as adoption) for the child.

It takes a village to raise a child.
—African proverb

6

COMING TOGETHER

M r. Frie was surprised to discover he was dealing with the welfare of two children. The fact that Mrs. Delaney was pregnant made it essential that she stop drinking immediately in order to reduce the risk of *fetal alcohol syndrome* to her unborn child. He explained this to Debra and spoke to her in more detail about the battered women's shelter.

"Even a short stay there offers some good benefits for you and your family, Mrs. Delaney. There are people on staff who can help you get started on your road to recovery, and it will give us some time to discuss the family's situation with your husband. Then we can all get together and decide the steps that need to be taken next."

"What about Ryan? Can he go there with me?" Debra asked.

"I think it will be best for Ryan, and for you too, if he remains at the Jefferson County Receiving Home while you get settled at the shelter, meet with a counselor there, and get started with Alcoholics Anonymous. Ryan is safe, but all this has been pretty traumatic for him. He's scheduled to meet with a psychologist tomorrow. Let's make sure that both you and Ryan are safe and getting the help that each of you needs. Then we can decide what has to be done to resolve everything else."

Debra agreed. She explained the arrangements to Ryan when he entered the room.

Ryan wasn't happy about living apart from his mom and dad, but he realized that his mother needed to be safe and needed help to stop drinking—especially after she told him about the baby. Ryan was shocked to discover he was going to have a little brother or sister. He knew from his health class at school that alcohol was extremely dangerous for an unborn child.

"How long will you have to stay at the shelter? Will I be able to see you?"

"We're not sure of the length of your mom's stay yet." Mr. Frie stepped in and responded to Ryan's questions. "But the two of you will definitely be able to visit each other often."

Ryan looked at his mom. "When are you going there?"

"Actually, someone at the hospital has already arranged it." Mr. Frie was the one who answered again.

Debra gave a shaky smile. "They tell me that I can move into the shelter today." She put her hand on her son's arm. "I've been thinking, Ryan; I hope this will be a turning point for us. I'm really sorry for everything that you've had to go through. I want you to know that I'm going to try really hard to make some big changes in my life so that we can be a real family again."

Ryan held back his tears as he said good-bye to his mother.

Mr. Frie arrived at the Delaney apartment Monday morning for his scheduled appointment with Tom Delaney. Tom admitted he had a problem controlling his frustration with Debra over her drinking and that his temper sometimes got the best of him. He expressed regret for hurting his wife and child, however, and for leaving Ryan alone with Debra on Saturday night. Mr. Frie asked if he would like an opportunity to discuss his situation with a ***clinical social worker*** and Tom agreed.

When Tom later told these same things to the clinical social worker, she explained the possible benefits of ***anger-management counseling*** and ***support groups***, and Tom decided to participate in both.

On Monday morning Ryan went to school, but not in the usual manner. There were never more than a dozen children at the Jefferson County Receiving Home, and a fifteen-passenger van dropped them off at both middle schools and the one high school in town. Ryan was concerned about not being able to take his regular bus to school because he knew Will and Jimmy would ask what was going on.

Ryan was not in the habit of always being truthful with his friends, and he had been wondering what kind of excuse he could come up with for this situation. Then he thought about what his mother had said yesterday at the hospital. "This could be a turning point for us," she had told him. Those words came back to him now, and he decided it was time to stop lying to his friends.

Mr. Frie visited the school later that afternoon to inform officials there of Ryan's temporary change of address and to interview Ryan's teachers concerning his behavior in school and any injuries they might have noted over the school year. He had told Ryan that it was part of his job to visit schools and talk to teachers, but he also explained how important confidentiality is to CPS. Ryan felt better about Mr. Frie's visit after the caseworker explained that he would not give the school any ***privileged information*** about Ryan or his family.

Things were moving very quickly, and Ryan's case was already being heard in juvenile court on Wednesday afternoon. Ryan didn't have to attend, but his parents were both there. His father had obtained the services of an attorney, who was also present. Mr. Frie filed a ***dependency petition*** describing some of the neglect and abuse that Ryan had endured. Ryan's parents admitted the allegations were true and expressed their desire to correct the situation. The judge agreed that custody of Ryan should be granted to the state, appointed a ***CASA volunteer*** to look after Ryan's best interests, and set a date for a ***disposition hearing***. He explained to everyone that at that hearing he would listen to the recommendations of CPS, the CASA volunteer, each of Ryan's parents, and anyone else that they deemed appropriate regarding the ***case plan*** for Ryan.

Debra spoke with Tom briefly after the hearing and was impressed to discover he had agreed to participate in anger-management counseling and to join a support group for men who had abused their wives. She had attended the battered women's support-group meeting at the shelter the previous evening and could already see the value in talking to people with situations similar to her own. Debra knew that drinking was a problem for her, but she was beginning to understand that it was never okay for Tom to strike her because of it. Debra knew he was wrong to hurt Ryan, even when it happened unintentionally. She realized that, like her, Tom needed help.

Meanwhile, Tom was happy to learn that Debra was determined to stop drinking. He knew she had a difficult road ahead of her, and he realized he had a lot of work to do himself. Tom understood that Debra would need assurances that he had his temper under control before she could leave the shelter and return home. Shame welled up inside him when he thought about the condition of his family. He berated himself for allowing it to get so bad that he could lose his wife, his son, and now his new baby.

He was already starting to realize that some of his problems had to do with his own low self-esteem. He was ashamed of the fact that he hadn't been able to get a decent job and provide for his family as he wanted to. When Mr. Frie told him about a special employment-assistance program available through the local Social Services office, Tom immediately scheduled an appointment with the employment counselor there. The clinical social worker had also suggested that Tom and Debra attend family counseling together, and both of them had agreed. Their first joint session would be next week.

Returning home after court, Tom took a good look at the apartment. Walking slowly from room to room, he felt embarrassed, just as he did when Mr. Frie visited him there yesterday. It seemed like this place was a **metaphor** for the mess he had made of his life.

How could I have gotten so angry with Debra for not cleaning when this is so overwhelming that I can barely tolerate the thought of cleaning it myself? he wondered. *How did everything get so far out of control? Why didn't I offer to help Debra sooner?*

There was much to do both to make the apartment livable and to change his life—but Tom was determined to tackle all of it, one step at a time. He filled the sink with water and began to take another step.

WHAT TYPES OF ASSISTANCE AND REHABILITATIVE SERVICES ARE PROVIDED TO FAMILIES BY CHILD PROTECTIVE SERVICES?

Many services are now offered to families in crisis. Some states make a distinction between the Office of Child Protective Services and the Office of Child Preventive Services. When a state has these two offices, CPS conducts investigations of child abuse and neglect and determines if a child can safely remain in the care of his family or if the child must be removed; Child Preventive Services is the office that works with the family to create a safe environment for the child's return. The reason for the creation of two offices is that some people believe a conflict can occur when one office is both the investigator and the helper of a family. In some states, initial investigations are turned over to police

The police work with Child Protective Services to ensure the safety of children.

The police and the court system may become involved once Child Protective Services has determined that child abuse has taken place.

Children need to feel safe, both at home and at school, in order to learn well and grow strong.

departments to reduce this role conflict. In other states, one caseworker from CPS will conduct the investigation and another caseworker from the same office will work to assist the family. Whether one or more offices are involved, various services are usually offered to the family after the family's needs are determined.

"It takes a village to raise a child," is a popular saying. In most communities there are churches, **nonprofit organizations**, businesses, and individuals who are ready to offer their knowledge and experience to families when called on to do so. When Social Services cannot provide a needed service directly, a referral to one of these agencies or individuals is often made. Services that might be offered to families include, but are not limited to:

- crisis intervention services
- foster care placement and oversight
- emergency shelter for children
- parenting classes
- financial assistance
- psychological counseling for both children and parents
- homemaker services (for example, instruction in how to properly clean and maintain a home)
- development of life skills (for example, instruction in how to shop for nutritious food and how to balance a checkbook)
- medical assistance
- mental health services
- treatment for drug and alcohol abuse
- educational programs
- employment counseling
- family counseling
- assistance and counseling regarding domestic violence
- assistance and counseling regarding sexual abuse
- anger-management counseling
- assistance in locating additional resources

ARE PROTECTIVE SERVICES FOR CHILDREN IN CANADA THE SAME AS THEY ARE FOR CHILDREN IN THE UNITED STATES?

Although there can be differences from one province to another, in general, the services for children in Canada are remarkably similar to those in the United States.

According to the Canadian Child Welfare Act, children are in need of protective services if their security, development, or survival is endangered due to any of the following:

- if the child has been injured physically (or if there is a substantial risk of this happening).

A child who is not adequately supervised is suffering from neglect.

- if the child has been sexually abused (or if there is a substantial risk that this will occur).
- if the child's guardian is unwilling or unable to provide protection for the child against sexual abuse or physical injury.
- if the child's guardian has injured the child emotionally.
- if the child's guardian is unwilling or unable to provide protection for the child against emotional injury.
- if the child's guardian has used cruel and unusual treatment or punishment against the child.
- if the child's guardian is unwilling or unable to provide protection for the child against cruel and unusual treatment or punishment.
- if the child's guardian is unwilling or unable to provide adequate care to meet the child's needs due to the condition or behavior of the child.

CANADA'S CHILD WELFARE ACT'S DEFINITION OF PHYSICAL INJURY, SEXUAL ABUSE, AND EMOTIONAL INJURY

Physical Injury

"A child is physically injured if there is substantial and observable injury to any part of the child's body as a result of the non-accidental application of force or an agent to the child's body that is evidenced by a laceration, a contusion, an abrasion, a scar, a fracture or other bony injury, a dislocation, a sprain, hemorrhaging, the rupture of *viscus*, a burn, a scald, frostbite, the loss or alteration of consciousness or physiological functioning or the loss of hair or teeth."

Sexual Abuse

"A child is sexually abused if the child is inappropriately exposed or subjected to sexual contact, activity, or behaviour including prostitution related activities."

Emotional Injury

"A child is emotionally injured if there is substantial and observable impairment of the child's mental or emotional functioning that is evidenced by a mental or behavioural disorder, including anxiety, depression, withdrawal, aggression, or delayed development, and if there are reasonable and probable grounds to believe that the emotional injury is the result of rejection, deprivation of affection or cognitive stimulation, exposure to domestic violence or severe domestic disharmony, inappropriate criticism, threats, humiliation, accusations or expectations of or towards the child, or the mental or emotional condition of the guardian of the child, or chronic alcohol or drug abuse by anyone living in the same residence as the child."

If we work together, we can make the world a
better place for each child.
—Georgia Holt

7

HELPING HANDS

As he washed the dishes, Tom thought about all the things that Mr. Frie and the social worker had told him. Life was getting better, he realized, but the apartment was as depressing as ever.

Even after it's clean, it's still going to look like hell. Cleaning isn't going to fix the peeling wallpaper or change the fact that the furniture is old and ripped. I don't have any money to change this. He felt defeated for a moment, but then he had an idea. *I'm capable of ripping the wallpaper off of the walls, but then what? I could paint them, but I don't have any paint or brushes. I wonder if I could talk the owner of the building into providing the paint if I donated all of the labor?* He decided to telephone the landlord, tell him about the condition of the apartment, invite him to visit so he could see what needed to be done firsthand, and offer to perform all the labor himself if the landlord would donate the necessary materials.

Tom had the apartment clean for the landlord's visit the next Saturday. Mr. Van Roy explained that he had not been in the apartment for years because he employed someone else to manage the buildings he owned. He was shocked to see the condition of the walls and floors and offered not only to purchase paint but also to replace the kitchen linoleum and the carpeting in other rooms. Tom was overjoyed; he couldn't wait to tell Debra, Ryan, Mr. Frie, and everyone else about his project.

Debra was also surprised to learn about the many services that were available to help her. She had begun attending Alcoholics

Anonymous (AA) and looked forward to her support group meetings. The shelter also offered employment counseling. Although Debra had finished high school, she had never held a job. She felt frightened and inadequate at the thought of even applying for one. "Who would even dream of hiring me?" she asked the counselor. "I've never had a job, and I'm not qualified to *do* anything. Besides, I'm about to have a baby. How will I be able to work with a baby to care for?"

"Everyone has to start somewhere, Debra," the counselor answered. "Each person who is employed today was once in the position of having to get her first job. You may not want to work when the baby is very young, but after that, there are many day-care options in town. A couple of employers even have day-care services on the *premises*. Debra, you've already told me that you were a good student. I think you should give some thought to the kinds of things that you're good at and to the various subjects that interest you. You'll need to take a course or two to develop and polish job skills, but we can arrange that. When you're ready, I'll help you write a resumé, and we'll practice making telephone calls to request an interview. Then we'll go over the kinds of questions that come up in job interviews and practice the interview itself."

By the time Tom and Debra began family counseling, they each had taken several steps toward improving their family life. The social worker was impressed that Tom had demonstrated his *initiative* by starting to remodel the family's apartment. She was also happy to hear that Tom's anger-management counseling was going well and that he had signed up for a parenting class.

Debra was also impressed, but she didn't feel ready to move back home yet. She wasn't confident of her ability to remain sober in an unsupervised setting, and after speaking with many of the women and her counselor at the battered women's shelter, she thought it would be best if Tom had more anger-management counseling sessions before they reunited. Debra wasn't just frightened about taking a possible drink or about Tom relapsing into rage; she understood how serious their custody situation was regarding Ryan. She wanted her son back, but when she got him back, she wanted it to be permanent. She didn't want to risk having CPS remove him from his home a second time.

She explained all this to the family counselor and to her husband. "I sure am anxious to see the apartment, though."

When Tom's employment counselor heard about the work he was doing on the apartment, he had an idea. "I see that you've also had quite a bit of carpentry experience in the jobs that you've had through the temporary employment agency. Do you enjoy that kind of work, Tom?" she asked.

Tom nodded. "I like working outside on projects, but I also enjoy the finishing work inside.

"Have you ever thought about doing volunteer work?" the counselor asked.

"*Volunteer* work? I need a real job, one that *pays me money*! I've got to find a way to support my family!"

"I realize that, Tom, and I'm going to help you find one. It's just that I don't know of any openings in construction right now, however, so I had another thought. Are you familiar with Habitat for Humanity?"

"They build homes for homeless people, right? I don't really know any details about it." Tom looked skeptical.

"They build homes for *qualified* homeless people, and the houses aren't completely free. Families who get Habitat homes have to work a number of hours to build homes for other people in order to qualify, and they usually have to pay Habitat something for the house. It's affordable because they don't pay for labor or interest, which makes monthly payments low. Anyway, I was thinking that volunteering to work with Habitat would give you an opportunity to continue fine-tuning your construction skills, you'd meet a lot of good people in the community, and you could begin building volunteer time with the organization that could help you if you and your wife decide to apply for a Habitat home at some point in the future. Besides all that, some of the people you'll meet might be involved in the construction business, and most jobs are acquired through **networking**. You have a lot of time on your hands right now, Tom, and there's nothing to lose by volunteering. Give it some thought; you might be surprised at the benefits it could bring to you. And even if nothing else comes of it, you'll have the satisfaction of knowing you helped someone."

Tom mulled over the counselor's suggestions. "Okay, I'll give them a call."

Mr. Frie had been a caseworker with CPS for a long time, and he'd worked with many different families. Over the years, he learned that some parents work very hard to regain custody of their children; others are immediately willing to give up permanent custody. He was happy to see the Delaneys putting forth such a ***diligent*** effort to regain custody of their son, and he really wanted them to succeed.

The case plan that he presented at the disposition hearing called for Ryan to remain in the custody of CPS on a temporary basis. The court agreed that Debra should continue with AA, and Tom needed to participate diligently in anger-management counseling. The court was pleased to learn that he was taking a parenting class. Additionally, Debra and Tom both agreed to continue with family counseling. The judge placed the decision regarding when to allow Ryan to move back in with his parents in the hands of CPS.

Two weeks after Tom told Mr. Frie about the work he was doing on the apartment, Mr. Frie decided to stop by for an ***impromptu*** visit and check things out for himself. He was impressed with Tom's work. The flooring hadn't been replaced yet, but the contrast between the gleaming new paint and torn old furniture was striking.

"I know what you're thinking," Tom observed when he saw Mr. Frie glance at the kitchen chairs. "I've been looking at those." He grabbed a chair and turned it upside down. "I can unscrew the seats right here. I'm going to buy some new fabric at that little store on the other end of the block, put it over the torn upholstery, and then just screw the seats back down. I don't know what to do about the living room furniture, though. I can fix the kitchen chairs, but big pieces of furniture are another story."

"I have an idea about that, Tom. Let me talk to a friend of mine at the Salvation Army, and then I'll get back to you." Mr. Frie hesitated and then continued. "There's another problem, Tom. I can tell you have a cat because of the odor in here."

"You're right. Butch is Ryan's cat. I don't know what to do to make him stop spraying indoors."

"Having him neutered might solve the problem. You need to give the local animal shelter a call, tell them you don't have the money to pay a large vet bill, and ask if they have a program to help low-income families get their pets neutered."

Tom made the call immediately. A few minutes later, Butch was scheduled for surgery.

Ryan continued to live at the residential facility because there was a shortage of foster families available locally. Moving him to another town would have meant a change in schools, and it would become more difficult to arrange visits with his parents. As things were now, he was able to see each of them at least once a week. Also, Mr. Frie and his coworkers had other cases that involved children who were certain to remain in the custody of CPS for a longer period of time than Ryan. The Delaneys were moving very quickly to improve their family situation, so Mr. Frie decided to place children whose situations were more desperate than Ryan's with the few foster families that were available in town.

Ryan wanted to return home, but he understood that his parents needed time to make their home and family life better. He was happy they were working on that while he had become comfortable staying at the Jefferson County Home. The staff members were nice, and he made friends among the other kids there. Everything was going well.

That's why he was so surprised when he got called down to the psychologist's office. A policeman was waiting to talk to him.

DO CHILD WELFARE WORKERS IN CANADA HANDLE CASES OF CHILD ABUSE AND NEGLECT IN A MANNER SIMILAR TO THAT IN THE UNITED STATES?

Yes, welfare workers and courts in both countries are charged with determining what is in the best interest of the child when investigating allegations of child abuse and neglect and deciding whether or not a child is in need of protection. To meet this obligation, each case is investigated and appropriate individuals are interviewed to determine the facts. As in the United States, Canadian caseworkers and courts have many options available to them when determining how best to assist a child and her family. When the safety of a child is in jeopardy, the Canadian government can become the legal guardian of the child. While the gov-

Canada and the United States have similar laws protecting children from abuse.

ernment has custody of the child, the child will be placed in a foster home or another residential facility, such as a group home or institution that caters to the special needs of that particular child. Both countries make an effort to keep siblings together.

Even when children are allowed to remain in the home, the child's parents may be asked to agree to a contract requiring them to participate in various programs aimed at improving the family situation. This could include, but is not limited to:

- Parents might be referred to community services offering various types of counseling, including family counseling or counseling and support groups for alcohol and drug abuse, anger management, or improved parenting skills.
- A home aide might be employed to assist the family in learning how to manage household tasks.
- Instruction might be provided in life skills such as budgeting.

Welfare workers in Canada can often assist the family in various ways, including:

- arranging for needed medical and dental care.
- helping to arrange day care.
- providing assistance in obtaining food, clothing, and housing.
- locating recreational programs for children.

The options available to and decisions reached by Canadian courts handling child custody cases are similar to those in the United States. The courts in both countries are reluctant to remove children from parental custody on either a temporary or permanent basis unless it is clearly in the best

Welfare workers help provide for the physical and emotional needs of children who have been abused.

interest of the child to do so. The following Canadian court orders are similar to those in the United States.

Supervision Order

Sometimes a child is allowed to remain in the home, but the child's situation is monitored by a caseworker from Social Services. Under this supervision order, the caseworker will check on the child on a regular basis and can remove the child from the home if the situation deteriorates.

Temporary Guardianship Order

When the Canadian government assumes guardianship of a child, the child becomes a Crown Ward. This can happen if a child has been physically or emotionally injured or sexually

A temporary guardianship order ensures that children who have been sexually, emotionally, or physically injured will have a safe place to stay.

abused in the home, and child welfare has determined that it is in the child's best interest to remove him from parental care and authority. The court may decide that the parents have to take certain specified actions and will set a time to review the case. At that point, the court may decide to return the child to the care and guardianship of her parents, extend the temporary guardianship order, replace that order with a supervision order, or make the temporary guardianship order permanent.

Secure Treatment Order

If a child is suffering from a behavioral or mental disorder that is severe enough to cause a threat to the child or to others, the court can use this order to confine the child to an appropriate facility for treatment.

If the court decides that the child can never return to her parents, she may be adopted into a new family.

Restraining Order

If a parent, guardian, or caretaker has caused emotional or physical injury or sexual abuse to a child, the court can issue a restraining order. This order makes it illegal for that individual to come in contact with the child.

Permanent Guardianship Order

If the court determines that the parents cannot, or are not willing to, make the necessary changes for return of their child, the court can decide to remove the child from the home on a permanent basis. Steps will then be taken to find a new permanent home for the child.

We need to give each endangered child
a priceless gift—hope.
—Letty Hoffer

8

A New Beginning

"Thanks for coming down, Ryan. Have a seat. This is Officer Martinez." Ryan's psychologist made the introductions. "He needs to ask you a couple of questions."

"Hello, Ryan. It's nice to meet you," Officer Martinez began. "First of all, I want to assure you that you haven't done anything wrong. That's not why I'm here. I also want to explain that I've met your parents, and they know I'm talking to you. The reason I'm here is to ask if you've ever met a man named Peter Walsh."

Ryan's head drooped forward as he stared at the floor. After a moment, he nodded his head.

"Ryan, I need you to tell me about Mr. Walsh."

Ever since Ryan had seen that magazine, he had tried really hard to *not* think about Mr. Walsh. Ryan hated to have to talk about that stuff now, but he also had come to understand that lying just made life more complicated.

Officer Martinez and the psychologist listened patiently while Ryan explained how he met Mr. Walsh and how Ryan worked for him until the day Mr. Walsh showed him the magazine with pictures of naked boys.

"What's going to happen now?" Ryan asked.

"I'm going to talk to Mr. Walsh," Officer Martinez explained. "I want you to understand that this is an official and confidential investigation, Ryan. You can talk about it to your psychologist and your parents, but not to anyone else."

111

"I already told my friends Will and Jimmy," Ryan said.

"That's okay," Officer Martinez answered, "but don't talk to them about it anymore until the investigation is complete. **Sexual exploitation** of children is a form of child abuse, Ryan, and it's against the law. It was wrong of whoever published that magazine to treat those boys that way. We need to discover who that was and make sure they don't do it again. Everyone who had anything to do with the manufacture, sale, or ownership of that magazine has committed a crime. It is wrong of Mr. Walsh to have the magazine, and it was wrong of him to show it to you."

Ryan felt relieved after he told the truth about Mr. Walsh. He had learned that it wasn't good to keep bad secrets. When the secret of his mom's drinking and his dad's anger became known, people were able to help them. *Maybe now someone will help Mr. Walsh and the boys in that magazine.*

After six weeks of being sober, Debra decided she was ready to return home. Tom was waiting on the balcony when the cab pulled into the alley. He ran down the stairs and opened the cab door. Debra was noticeably pregnant now, and Tom's concern for her was evident as he helped her out of the cab.

As she walked slowly up the stairs, Debra noticed that even the balcony had changed. A pretty new potted geranium bloomed between the plastic lawn chairs that had always been there. A book on parenting sat face down but open on one of the chairs, a sure sign that Tom had been reading.

Stepping into the apartment was an amazing experience. Debra's eyes filled with delight. Tom took his wife's hand and showed her all the changes he'd made.

Mr. Frie visited them at the apartment a few weeks later. He was happy to note that the apartment was well cared for. He already knew that both Debra and Tom were continuing to attend appropriate counseling and support groups, and he was pleasantly surprised to learn that Debra was also taking a computer class.

"How's your new job going, Tom?" Mr. Frie inquired. "You've been at it about a month now, right?"

"It's going great." Tom grinned. "You know it never would have happened if I hadn't volunteered at Habitat. Doing that was the best idea! It's really funny how one thing leads to another. One of the other volunteers told me there was going to be an opening at the place he worked. By the time I got there for an interview, he had already told the foreman about me. It was practically a done deal before I even filled out the application."

"I'm really happy for you, and I have some news I think you'll both like to hear." Mr. Frie looked at them both and smiled. "I recommended to my supervisor that Ryan be allowed to return home—and she's agreed."

Debra threw her arms around Tom. "When can we get him?"

"I can bring him here tomorrow afternoon. You need to understand, however, that although Ryan will be living here, CPS will continue to have custody. I'll be visiting from time to time."

"We understand," Tom replied. "We're just happy that he's coming home."

Ryan was excited yet nervous as he sat in Mr. Frie's car the following afternoon. It was strange to feel this way about going to your own home, but he knew that in many ways home was a different place now. *Different, but better*, he thought. The changes in his parents had been evident during his visits with them over the past weeks, but he couldn't stop the fear that nagged at the back of his mind. *Maybe all of these changes are just temporary*, he thought. *What if*

Mom takes a drink when I'm at school and Dad's at work? What will happen the next time Dad gets mad at Mom or me? Maybe all the positive changes would just fade away, the way his fantasies had always disappeared in the cold light of day.

His worries diminished, however, when he saw the beaming smiles on his parents' faces as they descended the stairs to greet him.

"We're so happy to have you home." His mom hugged him. Ryan couldn't help but notice her growing tummy, and he thought about how strange and wonderful it was that he would soon have a brother or sister.

"Let's take your things upstairs." His father placed his arm around Ryan's shoulders and gave him an affectionate squeeze.

Ryan thought about how many times he had dreamed of moments like this. He came to a quick conclusion that this reality was at least a thousand times better than any of his fantasies.

Ryan could barely believe his eyes when his proud parents took him on a tour of their remodeled apartment. The first thing Ryan noticed was how clean everything was, but then he saw that it was also pretty. He was surprised to see that the kitchen chairs had new seats and that a nice floral print sofa and chair now sat on brand new carpeting in the living room. "This is great!"

"Come and see what your father did in your bedroom, Ryan," his mother suggested.

Ryan was beyond happiness when he saw that his mismatched furniture had been painted a single color. "Everything looks so nice! Thanks! Hey, can I invite Will and Jimmy over? I want to show them where I live."

DIFFERENCES BETWEEN STATES REGARDING CHILD PROTECTIVE SERVICES

There can be many differences between states in the way that CPS is operated. Here are a few examples:

- In some states, cases are heard in family court rather than juvenile court.
- Some states operate residential treatment centers where parents and children can live together while the parents are working to improve parenting skills.
- Many states and welfare organizations employ "aides" or "homemakers" who visit families to help them improve safety, nutrition, cleaning, and shopping skills or to provide transportation. In fewer areas, these aides actually move into the home; in other states, families sometimes move into a foster home where they learn to model parenting and other skills from the foster parent.

Some cities have facilities that accept children at the parent's *discretion* on a temporary basis. A parent who feels that he is in danger of abusing a child can safely leave the child there until the danger passes.

SOME OF THE PROBLEMS ENCOUNTERED BY CHILD PROTECTIVE SERVICES

- Unfortunately, some individuals make frivolous calls to child abuse hotlines. The fact that CPS then has to investigate these calls takes time away from important cases.
- Sometimes families are subjected to an unwarranted and invasive investigation by CPS because a false accusation has been leveled against them.
- The system can move too slowly. Sometimes required timelines are not met. For example, the deadline to free a child for adoption may not be met because of required court dates and appeals.
- Investigating allegations of child abuse and determining whether or not to remove children from their homes is an extremely important job, yet the training and background requirements for caseworkers varies from one area to another.
- Some CPS offices have had difficulties in forming community partnerships for a variety of reasons. For example, organizations that are potential resources can be reluctant to become involved because of fear of *liability*, churches or other organizations may have limited financial resources, and the coordination of many community resources can be difficult and time consuming.

Suggestions for ways to improve Child Protective Services are often made. These include:

- In some localities, the relationship between Social Services and families is still considered to be too adversarial. Individuals suggest that in these areas more of an effort needs to be made to discover and build on each family's strengths.
- It has been suggested that professionals working in different aspects of child protection could benefit from **cross training** in order to better understand each other's jobs and develop improved working relationships. Some areas have already implemented

cross training (for example, between domestic violence workers and caseworkers for CPS).

- Being a caseworker for CPS can be a difficult and even dangerous job. In many locales, caseworkers have too many cases assigned to them, and each year many workers leave the profession. Some people have suggested that more funds should be allocated for the recruitment and training of caseworkers, and that experienced workers need to be rewarded in an effort to keep them on the job.

- Some people have suggested that all allegations of severe child abuse should be immediately referred to law enforcement officials for initial investigation. This would free up time and allow CPS to concentrate on assessing the needs of more at-risk families and locating services for them.

A SAMPLING OF INNOVATIVE CHILD PROTECTION PROGRAMS ALREADY BEING CONDUCTED IN SOME STATES

- Some community representatives and Social Services workers work together to develop new services for at-risk families and to correct problems with existing services.
- In some areas, CPS has turned certain duties over to other agencies that possess needed expertise. For example, public health nurses have been asked to perform assessments of drug-dependent newborns.
- Some states have offered special programs for **adolescent parents**; these programs have been successful in keeping both the parent and child safe and in limiting repeat pregnancies.

- In some areas, special dependency courts have been established for the purpose of referring drug-addicted parents to affiliated agencies for appropriate treatment.
- CPS staff members, along with other Social Services workers, such as employment counselors and health department personnel, sometimes establish offices in neighborhoods. This makes them more easily accessible to families who need services.

FURTHER READING

Atkins, Linda. *Jamaica and Me*. New York: Random House, 1998.

Bernstein, Nina. *The Lost Children of Wilder: The Epic Struggle to Change Foster Care*. New York: Pantheon Books, 2001.

Blue, Rose, and Corinne J. Naden. *Staying Out of Trouble in a Troubled Family*. Brookfield, Conn.: Twenty-First Century Books, 1998.

Corder, Cathy, and Kathryn Brohl, eds. *It Couldn't Happen Here: Recognizing and Helping Desperate Kids*. Washington, D.C.: CWLA Press, 1999.

Eldridge, Sherrie. *Twenty Things Adopted Kids Wish Their Adoptive Parents Knew*. New York: Dell Books, 1999.

Kemp, Allen. *Abuse in the Family: An Introduction*. Pacific Grove, Calif.: Brooks/Cole Publishing Company, 1998.

Libal, Joyce. *A House Between Homes: Youth in Foster Care*. Broomall, Pa.: Mason Crest Publishers, 2004.

Parent, Marc. *Turning Stones: My Days and Nights with Children at Risk*. New York: Random House, 1998.

Pelzer, David. *The Lost Boy: A Foster Child's Search for the Love of a Family*. Deerfield Beach, Fla.: Health Communications, Inc., 1997.

Richards, Keith N. *Tender Mercies: Inside the World of a Child Abuse Investigator*. Washington, D.C.: CWLA Press, 1999.

FOR MORE INFORMATION

American Humane Society
www.americanhumane.org

Childhelp USA®
www.childhelpusa.org

Child Welfare League of America
www.cwla.org

Medline Plus Health Information on Child Abuse
A service of the U.S. National Library of Medicine and the National
    Institutes of Health
www.nlm.nih.gov/medlineplus/childabuse.html

U.S. Department of Health and Human Services
Administration for Children and Families
www.calib.com/nccanch/

Publisher's Note:

The Web sites listed on this page were active at the time of publication. The publisher is not responsible for Web sites that have changed their address or discontinued operation since the date of publication. The publisher will review and update the Web sites upon each reprint.

GLOSSARY

anonymous: Without one's identity being know.

adolescent parents: Parents who are less than eighteen years of age.

allegations: Something that is declared to be true.

anger-management counseling: Counseling that helps individuals learn to deal with their anger in a way that does not harm themselves or others.

apprenticed children: Children employed by businesses or working as servants in order to earn money and learn a trade.

battered women's shelter: Temporary home for women (and usually their young children) who have been abused by their husbands.

CASA volunteer: Court-Appointed Special Advocate who is charged with looking after a child's best interests as decisions are made by Social Services and the courts regarding the child.

caseload: The total number of cases (children or families) being assisted by one Social Services worker.

case plan: The plan that is developed by a caseworker for a child and family.

clinical social worker: A social worker with a master's degree who is qualified to provide counseling and therapy.

confidential: Having to do with private information.

coroners: Public officers whose jobs consist of looking into the reasons for any death that may not have been due to natural causes.

cross training: Training in more than one discipline.

dependency petition: A document written by a caseworker and presented to the court alleging child abuse or neglect.

diligent: Showing consistent effort.

discretion: Individual's personal choice.

disposition hearing: Court proceeding where a judge will rule on child placement and other issues on a child's behalf.

escalate: Increase in intensity or severity.

exemptions: Exceptions to rules that others are subject to.

extended family: Aunts, uncles, grandparents, cousins; family members other than the nuclear or immediate family.

fetal alcohol syndrome: A dangerous medical condition that can affect babies born to women who drink alcohol while pregnant.

hearing: A preliminary examination of the facts in a criminal proceeding.

impromptu: Spur of the moment; without planning.

initiative: Energy displayed by starting a project.

intervention: Become involved in; to become a party in a legal proceeding involving others.

juvenile court: Special courts that deal only with cases involving youth.

liability: Something for which one is legally responsible.

mandated: Legally required.

medical indicators: Signs of abuse that doctors look for when performing a medical examination.

medical social worker: A social worker who is employed by a hospital and counsels patients concerning medical issues.

metaphor: Analogy, symbol; when something that is said or seen illustrates another concept.

networking: Getting to know an expanding group of people and using those contacts for purposes such as finding a job.

nonprofit organizations: Groups and charities that provide services without a profit motive.

paramount: Superior to others.

pornography: Text or images intended to cause sexual excitement.

premises: A particular building and the land that it is placed upon.

privileged information: Information that is of a private nature and not known to many people.

receiving home: Another name for a temporary shelter for youth.

ritual: A series of acts that is often repeated, such as that in a religious ceremony.

sexual exploitation: Improper sexual use of a person.

statistics: Collections of numeric data about a particular subject or group.

suppress: To stop; to keep down.

support groups: Groups of people with similar interests or conditions that meet on a regular schedule to share feelings and experiences and help each other deal with them in a positive way.

temporary custody: Legal and nonpermanent care of a person who is unable because of age or infirmity to be in charge of himself.

viscus: A soft internal organ, especially one within the abdomen.

INDEX

Adoption and Safe Families Act 22, 38
Adoption Assistance and Child
  Welfare Act 38
Alcoholics Anonymous 81, 97–98, 100
anger-management counseling 83, 84,
  98, 100

Canadian Child Welfare Act 90
Canadian Child Welfare Act,
  definition of physical injury, sexual
  abuse, and emotional injury 93–95
CASA volunteer 84
caseworker 68, 69, 71, 74, 75, 83,
  100, 102, 119
child abuse and efforts to protect
  children, history of 34–36, 38–39
child abuse and neglect laws, state
  exemptions in 32
child abuse and neglect, adult reasons
  that might foster 32
child abuse and neglect, adult signs of
  committing 25
child abuse and neglect, Canadian
  criteria for protective services 90, 93
child abuse and neglect, definition of
  18
child abuse and neglect, investigations
  in Canada 102, 104, 106
child abuse and neglect, investigations
  of 71–72, 74–75
child abuse and neglect, prevalence of
  16
child abuse and neglect, reporting of
  56, 58, 60, 63
child abuse and neglect, signs of
  22–23
child abuse and neglect, state
  definitions of 17

child abuse and neglect, state laws 32,
  34, 36, 58
Child Abuse Prevention and
  Treatment Act 17, 36
child pornography 55
child protection programs 120, 121
Child Protective Services (CPS) 56,
  57, 58, 66, 67, 69, 71, 72, 74, 75,
  77–79, 83, 84, 86, 88, 90, 99, 100,
  101, 113, 115, 120
Child Protective Services (CPS),
  between-state differences 115
Child Protective Services (CPS),
  problems encountered by 116
Child Protective Services (CPS),
  suggestions for improvement
  118–119
Childhelp USA® National Child
  Abuse Hotline 60
custody 67, 75, 78, 79, 100, 101, 104,
  107, 113

Department of Preventive Services 58,
  86
Department of Protective Services 58,
  86
Department of Social Services 23, 58,
  60, 84, 88, 120, 121
dependency petition 84

educational neglect 21
emotional abuse 18
emotional neglect 21

Fair Labor Standards Act 36
Family Preservation and Family
  Support Act 38
fetal alcohol syndrome 81

juvenile court 69, 115

mandated reporter 77
medical indicators 36
medical social worker 67, 69, 70

National Center on Child Abuse and
   Neglect 36
neglect 18, 20–21
New York Society for the Prevention
   of Cruelty to Children 36

order of protection 22

permanent guardianship order
   (Canada) 109
physical abuse 18
physical neglect 20

receiving home 68, 81, 83
restraining order (Canada) 109

secure treatment order (Canada)
   107
sexual abuse 45
sexual abuse, activities of 46–47
sexual abuse, prevalence of 45
sexual abuse, signs of 48
sexual abuse, what to do as victim
   51
Social Security Act 36
Stubborn Child Act 35
supervision order (Canada) 106
support groups 83, 84, 113

temporary guardianship order
   (Canada) 106–107

BIOGRAPHIES

Joyce Libal is a writer and artist living with her husband and assorted pets on their orchard in the mountains of northeastern Pennsylvania. When she is not writing, Joyce enjoys painting, quilting, and gardening. She has written several books for other Mason Crest series, including PSYCHIATRIC DISORDERS: DRUGS AND PSYCHOLOGY FOR THE MIND AND BODY AND CAREERS WITH CHARACTER.

Dr. Lisa Albers is a developmental behavioral pediatrician at Children's Hospital Boston and Harvard Medical School, where her responsibilities include outpatient pediatric teaching and patient care in the Developmental Medicine Center. She currently is Director of the Adoption Program, Director of Fellowships in Developmental and Behavioral Pediatrics, and collaborates in a consultation program for community health centers. She is also the school consultant for the Walker School, a residential school for children in the state foster care system.

Dr. Carolyn Bridgemohan is an instructor in pediatrics at Harvard Medical School and is a board-certified developmental behavioral pediatrician on staff in the Developmental Medicine Center at Children's Hospital, Boston. Her clinical practice includes children and youth with autism, hearing impairment, developmental language disorders, global delays, mental retardation, and attention and learning disorders. Dr. Bridgemohan is coeditor of *Bright Futures Case Studies for Primary Care Clinicians: Child Development and Behavior*, a curriculum used nationwide in pediatric residency training programs.

Cindy Croft is the State Special Needs Director in Minnesota, coordinating Project EXCEPTIONAL MN, through Concordia University. Project EXCEPTIONAL MN is a state project that supports the inclusion of children in community settings through training, on-site consultation, and professional development. She also teaches as adjunct faculty for Concordia University, St. Paul, Minnesota. She has worked in the special needs arena for the past fifteen years.

Dr. Laurie Glader is a developmental pediatrician at Children's Hospital in Boston where she directs the Cerebral Palsy Program and is a staff pediatrician with the Coordinated Care Services, a program designed to meet the needs of children with special health care needs. Dr. Glader also teaches regularly at Harvard Medical School. Her work with public agencies includes New England SERVE, an organization that builds connections between state health departments, health care organizations, community providers, and families. She is also the staff physician at the Cotting School, a school specializing in the education of children with a wide range of special health care needs.